Northumberland Aviation

CW00386491

Supplement & Update

INTRODUCTION

The intention of this supplement is to provide extra information and photographs to be added to my book, "Northumberland Aviation Diary", Aviation Incidents from 1790—1999, first published in 1999.

Where possible the full account of any incident has been included in the supplement, so as to apply a better conception of the events. For those people who bought the original book, I apologise for any repetition.

Acknowledgments

I am indebted to the following people and organisations for their assistance with information or photographs which made this book possible:

Tony Brown; J. Alan Hutchinson; Brian Outhwaite; G. E. Dickenson; Duncan Campbell; Gerry Newman; Bill Norman; Eric Nicholson; K. C. Peasgood; Steve Osfield; Peter Bolger; Dave Thompson; D. Wood; Brian Mennell; Stan Atkinson; D & P Harding; David Fenwick; Ron Bell; Dennis Curran; Joan Knowles; Andrew Howie; R. C. Fenwick; Theo Stoelinga; L. C. Morrison, MoD; Patrick Stevens Ltd; Berwick Advertiser; Hexham Courant; Newcastle Journal; Northumberland Gazette; Northumberland Weekend; "This England Books":- Mark Hawcroft; W. A. Ricalton; Geoffrey Books; Bill Fairbairn.

© Copyright Derek Walton 2005

Published By

NORAV PUBLICATIONS

3 Megstone Close
Seahouses
Northumberland
NE68 7XJ

First Published in 2005

ISBN 095361891 - 9

Typeset and layout by DESign
Printed and bound by
Martins the Printers
Berwick upon Tweed

In The Beginning

1800's

May/July 1825

Advertising poster for Ballooning on Newcastle Town Moor

Monday 15th August 1859

Account taken from "Evening Chronicle"

Early Stuntman's Trapeze Tragedy, Gymnastic Star died after balloon show error

William Henry Hall, Captain Hall to the public, was reckoned one of the top gymnasts of his time.

Hall, a dashing figure, who could pilot a balloon and swing from a trapeze hundreds of feet in the air was a sure-fire crowd-puller in the mid-1800s.

On Monday, August 15th 1859 he was a star in grand gala, promoted by first owner of the Victoria Music Hall, in Grey Street, Newcastle, a man called Smith.

A balloon ascent and a trapeze act, two death-defying stunts in one, guaranteed a vast turnout. Special trains were run to the city from as far away as Berwick, and on that fine summer night thousands had gathered at the old cricket ground in Bath Lane. It took three hours to inflate the balloon to lift the Captain aloft. Hall's balloon took him to around 1,000 feet, he climbed out of the basket as the crowd watched, spellbound.

A report, describing the scene said: "Hall got out and began a series of most extraordinary gyrations on the trapeze, holding on first by his hands and then by his feet.

"Women screamed and even strong men averted their faces, so it was quite a relief when the acrobat got back in the basket." Hall's problems had, however, only begun and would end fatally. The balloon began a series of alarming manoeuvres, floating down slowly and then rising at speed.

After some time the balloon rose higher and higher until it vanished from sight.

At 10.00 pm the cab driver hired to follow Hall's balloon returned to the cricket ground with the news. "The Captain had fallen from the balloon basket and was critically hurt at a house in Felling"

Mr. Smith and a surgeon dashed across the river and arranged for Hall to be taken to Newcastle Infirmary where he clung to life for three days before dying.

But how had the accident happened? Labourers in a nearby field who witnessed Hall's descent said, "Just as he was to step out of the basket the balloon suddenly rose rapidly. Hall's feet became entangled in the mooring ropes and, for several heart-stopping seconds, he hung suspended head down before falling 120 feet". The balloon was never seen again.

Hall's funeral, on the Sunday following his death, drew another vast crowd at Elswick Cemetery, in Newcastle.

1916

May 1916
Letter received from a Mr. Peasgood in 2004.
A British aeroplane came down at Long Riggs, West Sleekburn. It landed in a large field to the right as you travel from West Sleekburn Schools

1920's

Tuesday 12th November 1929
Page 18 of "Northumberland Aviation Diary"

Fairey Flycatcher S1285 of 408 Flt RNAS Donibristle. While flying through a snowstorm its engine cut, causing the pilot to force land at Yarrow near Falstone, Bellingham.

In doing so the aircraft upturned on landing without injuring the pilot, Lt/Cdr. I. R. Grant.

1930's

Wednesday 24th July 1935
Newspaper Report

Aeroplane made a force landing in a field near Brown's Farm at Cambois, Blyth, Northumberland. It had "City of Edinburgh" painted on its nose.

Note:- This was a three-engined Armstrong Whitworth Argosy of Imperial Airways.

1936

Walter Leslie Runciman (Later Viscount Runciman of Doxford) became Commanding Officer of 607 Squadron until 1939. He owned his own landing ground at Doxford Hall, near Chathill and was a prominent member of Newcastle Aero Club.

He was also Managing Director of BOAC and at the start of WW2 he was involved with the formation of the (Air) Ferry Service and the Air Transport Auxiliary

1939

Tuesday 10th October 1939
Page 22 of "Northumberland Aviation Diary"
1830 hrs.

Hawker Hart K6482 of 152 Sqd. RAF Acklington crashed on a ferry flight from Turnhouse to Acklington, when it flew into high ground near Cheviot . There was low cloud and rain about that day and Mr. Buchanan, a shepherd of Goldscleugh, saw the aircraft flying very low before it crashed into the northern slopes of Cheviot and burst into flames. He walked to Heathpool and raised the alarm . MR74/919221 Charred remains of pilot and machine were all that was left. Pilot:- 519466 Sgt. Thomas Mycroft, age 24 from Lewisham, London, is buried at Broomhill cemetery near Acklington.

Sgt.. T. Mycroft.

1940

Saturday 3rd February 1940
Page 33 of "Northumberland Aviation Diary"
1115 hrs.

Heinkel He111 H-3 1H-GK 2/KG26 was shot down into the sea 15 mile east of Tynemouth by Hurricanes of 43 Sqd Yellow Section, piloted by Sgt. F. Carey in L1726 and Sgt. Ottewill in L1849

Crew:-			
Obfw	F. Wiemer	Pilot	PoW
Fw	F. Schnee	Obs	PoW
Uffz	A. Dietrich	W/op	PoW
Uffz	W Wolff	Mech	killed
Uffz	K.E. Theide	A/G	killed

It was reported that F/Lt. C. B. Hull of 43 Sqd machine-gunned the survivors when they climbed onto the wing as it floated, but in fact, he only made a low pass intending to beat them up thereby causing them to jump into the water again. The Heinkel was said to have sunk within a minute.

Obfw. F. Wiemer.

Tuesday 2nd July 1940
Page 40 of "Northumberland Aviation Diary"
1745 hrs to 1800 hrs

This afternoon the Newcastle area sustained heavy air attacks leaving 15 people dead and 123 injured. Jarrow received most punishment with 14 people killed and many injured.

A German bomber obviously aiming at the Tyne Bridge, hit and badly damaged Spillers Factory situated nearby, killing one man, John Kelly age 28, of The Close, Newcastle upon Tyne.

Letter received from Mr Eric Nicholson

My wife's father, train driver Joss Goscombe was bringing a train across the High Level Bridge when, (as you report) his fireman spotted the German bomber which was probably aiming at either the Tyne Bridge or indeed the High level, actually hitting Spillers factory alongside the second bridge. – Joss saw the aircraft and as he said when talking about the event "I never drove a train so bloody fast over that bridge again."

4th September 1940
Air Raid 2315 hrs

12 Bombs exploded 300 metres SW of West Bitchfield, Belsay.

4 UXB discovered ½ mile north of Hartburn Village.

Tuesday 8th October 1940
Air Raid 2133 hrs

HE bombs fell at corner of RAF Cresswell and Cresswell road.

Thursday 10th October 1940
Air Raid 2029 hrs

UXB One fell in field at Laing Grove, Howden.

Monday 4th November 1940
Page 58 of "Northumberland Aviation Diary"

Spitfire Mk.1 L1094 of 610 Sqd RAF Acklington, was on a practice flight when the pilot lost control and the aircraft dived into boggy ground near Eglingham.

The pilot, 754486 Sgt. I M K Miller was killed.

Note:- At the request of his parents the RAF revisited this site in the 1950's to recover the remains of the pilot. He is now buried in Thame, Oxfordshire.

Further note:- A recovery dig was carried out on this site in August 2000 by Mike Davey and a team of enthusiasts from the newly formed North-West Aviation Heritage Museum at Hooton Park, Chester. Recovered was a Merlin engine, front windscreen, and other small parts.

Wednesday 11th December 1940

Spitfire Mk.1 P9451 & Spitfire Mk.1 X4649 both of 610 Sqd RAF Acklington collided south of Eglingham.

P9451 dived into the ground near Kimmer Lough killing the pilot:- Sgt. HB McGregor who was buried at Larkhill Cemetery, near Glasgow.

The pilot of X4649 :- P/O Ross bailed out successfully, his plane coming down on the banks of Titlington Burn.

1941

Tuesday 8th April 1941
Page 69 of "Northumberland Aviation Diary"

0430 hrs

Air Raid

4 HE fell, 3 of which exploded and 1 a UXB at South Moor Farm, Barmoor, Lowick.

Note :- Photograph supplied by Mr. Bill Fairbairn (now Deceased) who is seen at the time as a toddler standing with his mother.

Bomb Crater at Lowick.

Thursday 10th April 1941
Page 69 of "Northumberland Aviation Diary"

0001 hrs to 0449 hrs

Tyneside received its heaviest raid yet. An ambulance received a direct hit killing the female driver, Doris Ewbank aged 28 and attendant Edward Sutton aged 49.

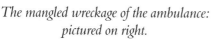
Doris Ewbank: pictured on left.

The mangled wreckage of the ambulance: pictured on right.

Friday 25th April 1941
Page 72 of "Northumberland Aviation Diary"

A.R.P. Report:-

Alarm sounded 2155 hrs to 2340 hrs

Major raid mainly on north Tyneside killing 70 people with several houses completely demolished at Heaton, Byker and Wallsend. Many unidentified casualties were later buried in a communal grave at Heaton cemetery.

Other raiders intent on attacking road and rail junctions, dropped an aerial mine damaging the railway crossing at Blyth Station, killing 51 year old John Norfolk and also 43 year old Isaac Brown of 7, Catherine Terrace. Further south near Seghill station, four people were killed also a mother and son at Shiremoor.

Letter received from Mr LV Edwards

When the Germans raided Blyth Station on 25/4/1941, my wife's Grandfather who was John Norfolk, together with his friend Isaac Brown could not go to the Air Raid Shelter, as they were waiting for a train to arrive and John Norfolk had to operate the signals.

They were on their way to the Signal Cabin when the mine landed killing them both, either inside the cabin or on the stairway.

I can remember people talking about the night it happened and they said rolling stock wheels were scattered over a wide area.

Saturday 3rd May 1941
Page 75 of "Northumberland Aviation Diary"

2312 hrs

Major damage was caused during a raid on Tyneside by 20 enemy bombers using HE and IB, some of which fell on Newcastle Town Moor.

2345 hrs

A tragedy occurred in North Shields when a direct hit on the basement shelter of Wilkinsons Lemonade Factory at the corner of King Street and George Street killed 103 people sheltering there. Heavy machinery on the upper floors crashed through into the basement.

Note:- To my knowledge no permanent stone memorial yet exists to those people who lost their lives, or to the rescuers who received medals in this largest single incident of loss of live caused by enemy action in Northumberland.

On 4th May 2003 a memorial metal plaque recording this tragedy was placed at North Shields Beacon Shopping Centre. The unveiling ceremony was attended by over 300 people including some of the survivors.

Friday 1st August 1941
Page 87 of "Northumberland Aviation Diary"

ARP Report:-

1530 hrs

One enemy aircraft dropped 3 HE bombs on the Longstone Lighthouse. Two of them almost direct hits, falling 20 yards and 30 yards away which put the engine room, turret and horn out of action. The kitchen was badly damaged. The third bomb fell in the sea.

Note :- The aircraft had waggled its wings similar to a friendly aircraft but came back and dropped its bombs.

On 31/5/2000 a machine-gun shell case from a German aircraft was handed into Bamburgh Castle Aviation Artifacts Museum by Mark Hawcroft, who had just discovered it on a sandy bay on Longstone Island.

Saturday 23rd August 1941
Page 90 of "Northumberland Aviation Diary"
2130 hrs

Heinkel He.111 H-5 Wk.No.3691 1H + EA of Stab/KG26 was one of six aircraft searching for a south bound convoy when it was hit by Ack Ack fire from an unseen destroyer. As it was unable to jettison its 500kg bomb it was forced to ditch into the sea north of Holy Island, Northumberland. The crew took to their dinghy and were picked up after 20 minutes and taken prisoner.

Crew:-

Hptmn	Georg Wilhelm	Pilot	PoW.	Deputy Staffekapitan
Uffz	Hans Hilbert	Obs	PoW.	
Uffz	Otto Siedel	W/op	PoW.	
Obgfr	Franz Schmidt	A/G	PoW.	

L – R: Schmidt, Hilbert, Wilhelm, Siedel.

Monday 1st September 1941
Page 91 of "Northumberland Aviation Diary"
Extracts taken from A.R.P. Report:-
2211 hrs

Junkers Ju.88 Wk.No.1064 4D+DB of Stab111/KG30. This aircraft had intended to raid Newcastle and was flying south from the direction of Ashington when it was intercepted by Beaufighter Mk.11 R2336 of 406 Sqd, RAF Acklington flown by F/O RC Fumerton RCAF with Sgt. LPS Bing as his A1 operator. The Beaufighter pilot obtained a visual against the moon, and despite erratic response from their A1 equipment they managed to close to firing range. Return fire from the Ju.88 was experienced but without inflicting any damage. On the second burst of fire from the Beaufighter, the enemy aircraft burst into flames and crashed into the Drying Sheds at Bedlington Brickworks, where the wreckage burnt furiously for three hours. Parts of the aircraft, including a complete dinghy, a compass, a belt containing five rounds of ammunition and also oxygen cylinders were recovered from fields over a wide area.

Mrs. Emily Surtees & daughter Margaret

The bodies of the crew were recovered from the wreckage two days later and placed in a shed at the brickworks by a team of RAF personnel from 63 MU, Carluke, Lanarkshire under the direction of F/O McKenzie. The German crew are buried in Chevington cemetery.

Crew:-

Obfw.	Helmut	Riede	Pilot	age 25
Oblt	Rudolf	Elle	Obs	age 29
Obfw	Helmut	Dorn	W/Opp	age 27
Fw	Walter	Muller	A/G	age 27

This was 406 Sqd's first victory as they were still officially non-operational.

Note:- The Tail Fin from this Ju.88 fell at the side of Brock Lane, Long Riggs and was placed on a lorry and taken to East Sleekburn Farm to await collection by the RAF, but was reported to have later been thrown into the mud of the River Sleek.

The Squadron scoreboard was made from a square of fuselage from this Ju.88 and the following appendix appears in the Combat Report. "The scoreboard is the personal property of Fumerton and is left with the unit on condition that if it is not desired by the War Museum, it will be returned to him."

Further Note:- Shown is a photograph I was sent of Mrs Emily Surtees and her daughter in their back yard holding a panel from the tail fin of this Ju.88. The V over the swastika was placed there by Mrs Surtees as a cymbal of defiance. The relic was later taken away by the recovery team.

Saturday 6th September 1941
1730 hrs

A. W. Whitley MK.V Z6932 ZA- 10 Sqd R.A.F Leeming. This aircraft had left its base the previous day on air test of it's instruments. Over the north sea the instruments had failed and due to poor visibility at its base, the aircraft was diverted to RAF Acklington but mistakenly landed at RAF Brunton, which was still under construction.

They were approached by three soldiers of the nearby Ack Ack site who informed them they were on the wrong airfield and that they only had to follow the railway line to find RAF Acklington or proceed further to Leeming. While attempting to take off the aircraft hit barrels on the runway, it swung and hit a steam-roller before becoming airborne again, but in trying to avoid high tension cables, hit them and burst into flames, stalled and crashed.

Rescuers, while battling against flames and flying bullets, broke the rear turret to extract the gunner who was in agony with back injuries. Five soldiers with their van were now in attendance, so the injured gunner was taken to a nearby farm before being removed to Newcastle General Hospital. Two of the soldiers later received Certificates of Commendation. (Sgt. Whitlock, the injured rear gunner, on his release from hospital returned to thank his rescuers)

Crew:-

F/Sgt.	William	Stuart	Pilot	R.C.A.F.	age 21	killed
P/O	Richard Scott	Austin	Pilot	RNZAF	age 21	killed
Sgt.	P. W.	Bryant	Obs	R A F		killed
Sgt.		Whitlock	W/Op-A/G	R A F		badly injured

Pilots' Stuart and Austin are buried at Broomhill, Acklington.

Note:- An eye-witness Mr. G. E. Dickinson was an army Ack Ack gunner at Brunton at that time and was involved in the rescue. A report he sent me stated. "On take-off the aircraft had first hit a barricade across the end of the runway made up of Barrels with Planks laid on top."

Tuesday 9th September 1941

Spitfire Mk.11a P7751 72 Sqd RAF Acklington. Hit pill box on approach to land killing the pilot.:- 1290143 Sgt. J.M. Coxon.   Grave at Harton Cemetery, South Shields.

Friday 21st November 1941
1600hrs

Hurricane Mk.1 V7425 AU-V 55 OTU RAF Usworth. Pilot was lost with low fuel, so landed with undercarriage down at Ulgham Manor Farm, 6 mile S of Acklington, damaging airscrew, wings and undercarriage.

Pilot:- 567030   Sgt.   J.   Goldney.   uninjured

1942

Sunday 3rd January 1942
Page 101 of "Northumberland Aviation Diary"
Account taken from "Berwick Journal":-

A daring raid by a single Nazi plane, resulted in the death of four persons in a North East Coastal town. *(Berwick & Tweedmouth).*

A father, mother, married daughter and a school attendance officer were wiped out in the bombing attack, which was proceeded by a fierce low-level machine-gun raid. The lone raider took advantage of low cloud to make the attack on the town.

Killed in the demolished house were Mr J.H. Harvey age 36, Mrs Wallace age 25, also Mr & Mrs W. Younger ages 53 and 52. *Mr. & Mrs. Younger's Budgie lived through this bombing.*

Friday 30th January 1942
Hurricane Mk.1 V7425 AU-W 55 OTU RAF Usworth. Force landed in a field near RAF Tranwell. Pilot lost contact with his station and was forced down in bad weather.
Pilot:- R62844   Sgt.   La Pointe.   RCAF slight injuries.
1100hrs
Hurricane Mk.1 V7613 PU-W RAF Usworth. Engine failure caused by seized bearings resulting in an engine fire, forcing the pilot to make a crash landing on the south west corner of RAF Morpeth damaging the undercarriage and propeller.
Pilot:- J8324 P/O   Patterson.   RCAF

Friday 1st May 1942
Page 107 of "Northumberland Aviation Diary"
0234 hrs to 0402 hrs

Raid on Newcastle leaving many dead.

Bombs killed 18 people in Newcastle and Wallsend, causing damage to dwelling houses and a Tanker on the river.

One bomb demolished houses at No. 12 and 13 Coley Hill Terrace, North Walbottle, killing William Musgrove age 54. His daughter Dora age 20 and a neighbour Margaret Allen, were seriously injured and both died later that day in hospital.

0402 hrs

A German raider chased by a fighter jettisoned its bombs over Bolam Church. One bomb went under the church by penetrating a pathway outside the church wall, but did not explode. The bomb was later removed. It had been released from very low level and probably did not have time to arm itself.

Willi meets the locals.

Note:- A stained glass window has been installed at this point in the wall recording the event.

Further Note:- Bill Norman author of several books concerning German air activity over the North East, recently researched this event for a new publication and discovered the name of the pilot involved, from whom he obtained the following facts.

The aircraft was a Do.217 from KG/2 and during a raid on Sunderland, he was intercepted and attacked by a Beaufighter from Corby Grange.

To escape the nightfighter the Do.217 pilot Fw.Willi Schludecker dived his plane into clouds. On coming out below the cloud, as he thought over the sea, he was amazed to see trees on either side of him, one wing taking the top off a tree 50 metres south of the Church. By this time it was decided to jettison the 4 x500Kg. bombs, whereupon they straddled the Church of St Andrews at Bolam, one exploding in the vicarage garden, another UXB finishing up under the Church and two more exploding 3 & 4 hundred metres north in fields.

On Monday 12th July 2004 Bill Norman arranged for Willi, the German pilot, to revisit Bolam Church and meet some of the people he frightened 62 years ago. It was a great success with no hard feelings on either side.

Sunday 10th May 1942
2030hrs

D. Havoc Mk.1 AW 392 1460 Flt RAF Ouston - det: from RAF Swanton Morley, was on a practice interception flight at 12,000ft when the port engine cut and the aircraft glided down to 2,000ft. Leveling out, the pilot opened full starboard engine which pulled the aircraft into a spin. The spin stopped at 100ft then the aircraft dived into ground on a railway embankment at Mossy Ford Farm, two mile south-west of Alnwick, killing both crew and bursting into flames. An eye-witness stated that the Havoc was trailing smoke from one engine and was being accompanied by one Hurricane.

Crew:-

6755862 Sgt. M. M. Kent Pilot killed. Buried at Craigton Cemetery, Glasgow, Section T. Grave 933

1066010 Sgt L. Lucas Obs. killed. Buried at Kirkdale Cemetery, Liverpool, Section 7. Grave 1391

Tuesday 11th August 1942
Page 113 of "Northumberland Aviation Diary"
0130 hrs

B.17 E Flying Fortress FK204 (Ex USAF 41 – 9198) of 220 Sqd RAF Ballykelly, Northern Ireland. While on patrol was lost and out of fuel, so auto-pilot was engaged and the crew abandoned the aircraft over Kelso. The aircraft then flew on and crashed 900 yards (metres) south east of Doddington Quarry near Wooler.

Thursday 20th August 1942
1435hrs

Master 11 AZ501 of 8 FTS RAF Montrose. On flight from base to RAF Woolsington when shortage of fuel caused it to force land at Rothley Craggs, Cambo, causing slight damage to undercarriage and propeller. Pilots uninjured.

1st 959172 Sgt. HT Allen
2nd 1335046 Sgt. TH Debenham

Sunday 11th October 1942
Page 115 of "Northumberland Aviation Diary"
1400 hrs

Hurricane Mk.1 V6733 of 59 OTU RAF Milfield, crashed near Elwick, north east of Belford. The pilot Sgt. Wilson RCAF had bailed out successfully.

1943

Saturday 16th January 1943

Hurricane Mk.1 AG 181 of 59 OTU RAF Milfield when low on approach to base just north of the village, the engine cut and caught fire. This caused the aircraft to touch down in a field and run on for 50yds before crashing through a strong hawthorn hedge. It came to rest 50 yds further on where it burst into flames near Milfield Village killing the pilot.:- 1388453 Sgt. James Henry Hobbs age 20, buried at Kirknewton.

Tuesday 23rd February 1943

Beaufort DX118 While on ferry flight, crashed in bad weather near Chew Green, north of Byrness. The ATA (Air Transport Auxiliary) pilot :- First Officer William Byrd Lee Milton of USA was killed in the crash.

Monday 1st March 1943
1515hrs

Wellington Mk 1c X3171 15 OTU RAF Harwell. Took off 1100hrs on a cross country flight and while flying in cloud, control was lost and it dived into the ground near Ridley Shiel, Comb Hill, 9 mile north west of Bellingham, killing all crew. Sgt. Gibson was from Newcastle-upon-Tyne.

Crew:-

1337932 Sgt.	D L	Barley	Pilot	killed	
1526809 Sgt.	W S	Gibson	Nav age 20	killed	Grave at Stamfordham
132810 P/O	J	Donnelly	B/A-A/G	killed	
134723 P/O	G	Winstanley	B/A-A/G	killed	
1197228 Sgt.	D R	Bending	W/op-A/G	killed	
1096256 Sgt.	G	Marshal	A/G	killed	Grave at Trimdon Grange

Wednesday 5th May 1943
Page 126 of "Northumberland Aviation Diary"
1405hrs

Hurricane Mk.1 R4188 of 59 OTU RAF Milfield. When flying in cloud and out of fuel, crashed in forced landing besides the Observer Post at Chatton.

Pilot:- 142503 Sgt. George Renshaw slightly injured.

1530hrs

Spitfire Mk.11 P7902 57 OTU RAF Eshott was hit by Hurricane AG111 and both crashed near Wooler on Doddington Fell killing the two pilots. The Hurricane had dived on the Spitfire which was flying in a formation.

Pilot:- 416496 Sgt. Fergus T.O. Hulton RNZAF age 19 killed. Buried at Broomhill.

Hurricane X AG111 59 OTU RAF Milfield collided with Spitfire P7902 and crashed as above.

Pilot :- 1393813 F/Sgt. HA de Freitas age 26 Buried at Wellshill, Perth, Scotland.

Monday 10th May 1943
Page 127 of "Northumberland Aviation Diary"

Botha Mk.1A L6531 of 4 AGS RAF Morpeth, flew into a hillside in a freak snowstorm at Hazeltonrig near Rothbury, killing the three crew. Two other aircraft caught in this storm managed to land at RAF Boulmer.

781582 Sgt.   S Zawilinski   (Poland) Pilot   age 23 Grave at St.Mary's, Morpeth

1161843 LAC D Campbell   U/T A/G age 27 Grave at Allesley, Coventry

2215993 LAC K Bradley   U/T A/G

1001939 LAC H Carter   U/T A/G

L.A.C. Duncan Campbell.

Note:- I visited this site in 1978, all that remained was a burnt patch on the rocks. Many thanks go to Mr Duncan Campbell of Chile, nephew of crew member, for sending e-mail of photograph and extra details

1944

Tuesday 29th February 1944
1230hrs

Sea Hurricane 781 Sqd RNAS Lee-on-Solent. Crashed in a field at Fowberry Moor Farm, Chatton, during a heavy snowstorm and bad visibility.

Pilot :- Lt/Cdr AF Hall age 35 uninjured.

Friday 3rd March 1944
1150hrs

Spitfire Mk.V EP143 of FLS RAF Milfield. Engine cut on take-off and crashed at Yeavering Farm, Kirknewton.

Pilot:- 30459 S/L Jean Yourmer FFAF was slightly injured.

Tuesday 7th March 1944

Spitfire V EP550 of 222 Sqd RAF Acklington. Crashed while low flying and flew into a stone wall south of Lemmington Branch, 1½ mile NE of Edlingham killing the pilot :-
791193 F/Sgt. J. M. Morris of South Africa, age 21, buried at Broom Hill, Acklington.

Tuesday 11th April 1944
Page 139 of "Northumberland Aviation Diary"

Spitfire Mk.X1V NH 700 of 322 Sqd RAF Acklington dived into Dove Crag, Tossen Hill, near Whitton, Rothbury.

Pilot:- 132085 F/O Jacob Willem Van Hamel (Dutch) age 23 killed, grave at Broomhill.

Note:- During 1997 the sister and niece of the pilot came across from Holland to visit his grave. It appears the pilot was involved in the removal of a traitor in the Dutch resistance, he then escaped from the Nazi occupying force by crossing the North Sea in a canvas canoe. On reaching Britain he joined the RAF and eventually trained to fly Spitfires. It was while flying on an errant to obtain spare parts that he crashed into the hill.

Monday 5th June 1944
Page 140 of "Northumberland Aviation Diary"

H. Typhoon Mk.1b R7822 3 TEU RAF Acklington, engine cut at low altitude and caught fire. Pilot carried out an excellent forced landing with wheels up and flaps down at Low Newton, at the rear of The Ship Inn, 3 mile south of Beadnell. Unfortunately the pilot had the hood closed and it was impossible to release him owing to the fierceness of the fire.

Pilot :- 1387068 W/O J.S. Gilbert killed.

RAF Enquiry Comment :- Always land and take off with the hood in the open position as this pilot could have been saved if the hood had been in the open position.

Letter from Mr. Stan Atkinson *who was an airman stationed at RAF Boulmer at the time of the crash. He was one of the Crash Guard attending this incident and was camped on site for three days until the pilot was taken away and the wreckage removed. Each year on the 5th June he attends a reunion at the above mentioned Pub in memory of the pilot.*

Saturday 24th June 1944
Page 141 of "Northumberland Aviation Diary"
1145hrs

Spitfire Vb EN794 of FLS RAF Milfield. This aircraft had taken part in practice bombing at the North Dive Screen at Doddington, but later while carrying out air to ground firing practice it crashed at Goswick Ranges. The pilot, Lt/Cdr D. R. B. Cosh DSO RCNVR HMCS "Niobe" was killed.

Note:- The pilot had been CO of Royal Navy 881 Sqd from November 1943. His burial took place at 1420 hrs on 27th June 1944 at Kirknewton cemetery, where his squadron dedicated a beautiful stained glass window to him in the north wall of the church.

Lt/Cdr D.R.B. Cosh

Saturday 19th August 1944

Sea Hurricane 1A BW855 731 Sqd RNAS East Haven. (HMS Peewit), Tayside. Was on a ferry flight to RAF Sealand in Wales when it struck high ground 4 mile south of Hepple near Rothbury, killing the pilot.

Saturday 30th September 1944

Spitfire Mk.11a P7884 57 OTU RAF Eshott collided in the air with Spitfire AR 697 of the same unit. Both aircraft crashed in the sea 2 mile off Druridge Bay.

The pilot F/Lt McNair-Taylor was killed.

S/Ldr Shaw pilot of the other Spitfire involved bailed out into the sea.

Letter from Mr R. Bell

The incidents you record involving aircraft from 57 O.T.U. Eshott during 1944 were of particular interest, as I served there as a Flying Control Officer, and on duty when those of Wednesday 12th April, and Monday 19th June, occurred. The collision on 30th September, was particularly memorable, as the formation was not expected to cross the coast, so the pilots were not carrying dinghies. When it was known that our C.F.I. (Chief Flying Instructor) Johnnie Shaw, was in the sea, reported floating in his "Mae-West, - as Air Sea Rescue Officer, I suggested scrambling an aircraft with the intention of dropping a dinghy. - I got the job!, and with S/L Bedford as pilot, flew out to Druridge Bay and on the way, discussing how to achieve the desired result. In the event, we saw that S/L Shaw had been picked up by local fishermen, and was in a boat being rowed ashore. A great relief in more ways than one, as it had been decided that, if the attempt to drop the first dinghy failed, I was to parachute down with a second one!

Johnnie Shaw told me afterwards that, having lost control of his aircraft in the collision, he was having difficulty baling out, and pulled his chute in the cockpit, scooping up the silk and pushing it into the slipstream. He was, literally, "snatched" from the aircraft, performing a back-somersault, which dislocated his shoulder. We later met-up at Thornaby, where he was serving as Station Commander in 1951. He recalled that event as the "most hairy" of his many airborne experiences. Eshott sticks in my mind as the busiest airfield on which I served, with rarely a day going by without some emergency.

1945

Wednesday 28th February 1945
Page 154 of "Northumberland Aviation Diary"

B. Beaufighter Mk.V1F ND226 54 OTU RAF Charter Hall. Aircraft filled with petrol fumes and port engine failed causing the aircraft to loose height. The pilot was unable to force land as the windscreen was covered with oil, so crew bailed out. The aircraft landed by itself at Low Ardley, 4 mile south of Hexham.

Crew:- 542651 F/Sgt. JM Harvey the pilot and his R/O sustained minor injuries

Note:-In 1979 I visited the site and learned that the aircraft had been taken away on a Queen Mary trailer by a recovery crew, but only after a stone wall had been dismantled. The gentleman who gave me this information was using an old airfield control van in his garden as a shed.

Wednesday 18th April 1945

Spitfire Vb AA920 57 OTU RAF Eshott. Broke up in the air during aerobatics and crashed 1 ½ mile NW of Longhorsley near Viewlaw Farm,.This aircraft had a long history.

Crew:- F/Sgt. EK Pannett age 21 killed

Monday 7th May 1945
Page 156 of "Northumberland Aviation Diary"
2300 hrs

One hour before the formal German surrender took place, the submarine U2336 Type XX111 boat, under the command of Kapitanlautnant Emil Klaus Mayer intercepted a convoy one mile east of May Island. He sank two ships, the "Evendale Park" and the Norwegian "Sneland 1" before successfully returning to Germany to surrender. Nine men were pointlessly killed. Thus it was the Firth of Forth, and in particular May Island, which saw both the very first and the very last enemy action against mainland Britain during the second world war.

German U-boat Command passed an order to all U-boats on the evening of 4th May that all German submarines were to observe a cease-fire with effect from 0800hrs German Time the following morning. All attacks were forbidden and any current pursuit was to be abandoned forthwith. All attack U-boats were to return to Norwegian harbours.

1946

Tuesday 23rd July 1946
Page 158 of "Northumberland Aviation Diary"

V.A. Warwick Mk. ASR V1 HG 136 280 Sqd RAF Thornaby was en-route from base to RAF Brackla to be scrapped. While flying north it hit the west summit of Cheviot, at Cairn Hill. MR 80/899196 The aircraft had been operating with 269 Sqd shortly before this, in the Azores.
Note:- It was three days before the aircraft was found. The first news of the crash came from hill walkers John Daly, John Miller and Robert Pitts who were Tyneside Engineering Apprentices and spotted the wreckage on Hen Hole Peak early evening. They reported it to Mr. and Mrs Cowans who farmed Mount Hooly Farm in the College Valley. Mr Cowans and two friends set out to find the crash guided by the smell of burning oil and found only 2 bodies.
Airmen from RAF Acklington then commenced a search for the remaining member of the crew who was unfortunately dead when discovered.

Crew:-

	F/O	Herbert Arthur	Cody	Pilot	killed
160576	F/Lt	Dennis Thomas	Chadd	W/Op A/G	killed Grave at Broomhill
	F/Lt	Kenneth Fredrick	Wyett		killed

On 16th June 1998 a helicopter from RAF Boulmer was carrying out an exercise in that area and recovered the starboard tailplane and part of the rear fuselage from this crash site. These items are now on display in BCAAM (Bamburgh Castle Aviation Artifacts Museum).
RAF Brackla was three mile SSW of Nairn, Scotland with a 2000m NE – SW grass runway. From 1945 until 1947 it was used as 102 Sub Store as part of 45 MU RAF Kinloss for scrapping aircraft, mostly Halifax.

1947

Wednesday 17th September 1947
Page 160 of "Northumberland Aviation Diary"

Mosquito Mk.NF38 VT587 of 2 APS (Armament Practice School) RAF Acklington.
While carrying out a slow roll during practice for a Battle of Britain Display, the aircraft stalled and crashed near the base.

Crew:-

50808	F/Lt	D	Byrne	Pilot	killed
	F/O	C	Johnson MB BS	Passenger	killed

Letter received from Mr Eric Nicholson

I attended my demob medical at RAF Acklington on that Wednesday 17th and was examined by F/O Johnson. On my entering the Examination Room he explained he would not take very long with me, for he was due to achieve an ambition and fly in a Mosquito immediately after my medical examination. Sadly the aircraft crashed in an adjacent field after completing a manoeuvre and stalling.

1948

Tuesday 1st April 1948
Page 160 of "Northumberland Aviation Diary"

Anson Mk. 19 TX194 of 13 Group Communications Sqd RAF Ouston, ran out of fuel and crashed in a forced landing five mile west of RAF Ouston.

Letter and photograph from Mr D Wood stating :- *"The aircraft landed in a field about half a mile or so south of Stagshaw crossroads on the western side of the A68."*

Avro Anson. Crash hear Stagshaw.

1949

Monday 27th June 1949

Martinet TT1 NR 300 APS RAF Acklington. Engine ran rough and was switched off, belly-landing on Brunton disused airfield.

Sunday 4th December 1949
Page 161 of "Northumberland Aviation Diary"

Spitfire F22 PK315 607 Sqd RAF Ouston. Dived into the sea off Seahouses from high altitude formation killing the pilot. P/O Leslie Oates. It was presumed the pilot lost consciousness.

Further note:- On Friday 18th March 2005, Neil Priestly a fisherman from Seahouses with his boat, "Portia of Pool", recovered a four hollow bladed propeller off the Fame Islands. It most probably belonged to this aircraft and is now on display at Bamburgh Castle Aviation Artefacts Museum.

1950

Tuesday 24th January 1950
Martinet TT1 RG907 2APS RAF Acklington. Undershot when engine cut on approach to base and crash landed.

Thursday 20th April 1950
Mosquito FB6 RS528 23 Sqd RAF Church Fenton. During bombing practice, spun in off a turn and dived into the sea in Druridge Bay, killing two crew.

Saturday 24th June 1950
Spitfire F22 PK394 607 Sqd RAF Ouston. Dived into the sea out of cloud 40 mile off Blyth, killing the pilot.

Sunday 20th August 1950
Spitfire F22 PK393 607 Sqd RAF Ouston. Ran out of fuel on exercise in bad weather and undershot forced landing near Boulmer injuring the pilot.:- F/O D Curran.

Spitfire F22 PK595 607 Sqd RAF Ouston. While on exercise with three other aircraft, ran out of fuel and although the pilot attempted to bale out the aircraft crashed at Knipe Scar, 3 mile south of Hackworth, Westmoreland causing a crater 10 feet (3 metres) deep and scattering wreckage over a wide area. Unfortunately the pilot,:- Sgt. E A (Ted) Carter was killed.

Letter from F/O Dennis Curran. *As I remember, the weather that day was poor with low cloud but the C.O., Tony Dunford, judged it was safe to fly. There were four of us with me leading the formation – the purpose of the exercise escapes me – but before long the weather clamped down as we used to say in those days and we quickly attempted to return to base.*

We flew east to make a safe descent over the sea then followed the Tyne up river to locate Ouston. There was just enough of a window to allow numbers 3 and 4 to make a safe landing but by the time our turn came the cloud was at ground level, so we had to abort and seek direction to another field and this is where the problems started.

The Ground Control Centres seemed to have had difficulty getting accurate fixes on us and a series of conflicting messages and directions were transmitted. During the course of this confusion my number two, who had been in close formation all the time, suddenly veered away. I was unable to establish R/T (Radio Transmitter) contact with him and that was the last I saw of him. Later I was told that he had crashed in the Lake District, killing himself in the process. He was only a young chap.

After flying seemingly fruitless courses for some time I ran out of fuel, sent out a Mayday and prepared to bale out. Fate then played its hand. The fickle finger opened the tiniest gap in the cloud through which I could vaguely see what appeared to be a runway. I had by this time undone my straps. I managed to negotiate the gap with a dead engine, gliding to a forced landing, smashing my head on the gunsight and a couple of fields away from the runway. I think it was Boulmer. I was picked up by a couple of chaps out shooting and driven to Alnwick Hospital, not that I remember anything of that. The outcome was a fractured skull, a few bruises and the end of my flying career.

Sunday 3rd September 1950
Spitfire F22 PK498 607 Sqd RAF Ouston. On approach to base one wing dropped causing it to spin into the ground inverted, killing the pilot.

1951

Friday 16th February 1951
Page 161 of "Northumberland Aviation Diary"

Meteor F8 VZ498 245 Sqd RAF Horsham-St-Faith. Ran out of fuel after compass failed on air-to-air firing exercise and crashed near Whittingham west of Alnwick. The pilot was carrying out a force landing when the aircraft hit a tree and was inverted. The pilot, F/Lt Adams was killed when he attempted to eject from the aircraft. His body was sent home to Glasgow by train for burial.

Incident worth recording

Taken from a book "Spitfire Against The Odds" (Patrick Stephens Ltd. ISBN 1-85260-247-3) written by R.A. Ashman who at one time served post-war as a Sergeant Pilot with 607 Sqd while at RAF Ouston. The following incident was while he was flying a Harvard.

"I was glad to pick up where I left off and went solo one day on a cross-country exercise. I flew up to Berwick and beat up my old homestead, leaving, I shook up the town by flying up river under the two bridges, and through the arches, just for the devil of it."

(Author):- At least once a week when I visit Berwick I always look at these bridges and wonder "How was it done?" !! A Harvard has a wingspan of 42 feet.

North American Harvard.

Berwick Bridges.

1952

Wednesday 22ⁿᵈ October 1952
Page 163 of "Northumberland Aviation Diary"

Meteor F8 VZ461 43 Sqd RAF Leuchars. When its artificial horizon failed, the aircraft dived into the sea out of cloud off Amble killing the pilot.

1953

Friday 17ᵗʰ April 1953
Page 163 of "Northumberland Aviation Diary"

Meteor F8 VZ501 72 Sqd RAF North Weald. While detached to RAF Acklington, flew into the sea out of cloud 2 mile east of Coquet Island, killing the pilot.

Thursday 7ᵗʰ May 1953
Page 164 of "Northumberland Aviation Diary"

Anson Mk.T21 VV299 of 11 EFTS (Elementary & Reserve Flying Training School) RAF Perth, Perthshire, hit trees while turning in bad visibility and crashed six mile west-north-west of Alnwick.

Letter from Mr Tony Brown :- *At the time I was an eleven year old digging the garden with my father at Glanton, when the Anson flew past to the south of the village from west to east. It was low, but not at an unusually low altitude and had been round once or twice before. I heard the steady drone of the engines as it disappeared around Glanton Hill, then the noise stopped with a –Boom. I said to my father, I thought the plane had crashed and I was told – not to be so silly. A short time later my mother, who was the district nurse, came to our house saying that a plane had crashed and we had to go to the crash site to help.*

We all got into the car, a Ford Anglia, and drove to the crash site on the side of Titlington Pike. When we got there I was immediately puzzled by the position of the aircraft. It was in the corner of a field pointing down hill and parallel to the length of the field. Its tail was close to one edge of the field and the left wing close to the other edge of the field, but trees behind the tail totally undamaged. The aircrew were walking around the aeroplane and I don't believe anyone was seriously injured. My mother attended to them and I think we took the worst injured – a broken arm – to Alnwick infirmary. I remember going into the aircraft and seeing a sextant on a table.

The reason for the crash we were told from the crew, was, that the plane had been on a training flight from Glasgow to Liverpool. The pilot's wife was staying at a farm close by, and he thought it would be a nice surprise to drop in and see her. The pilot had been trying to land in the next field but his right wing had struck the trees and so dropped his left wing which had dug into the field and spun the plane through 180 degrees where it had come to a stop. That explained the undamaged trees just behind. However I am certain that it wasn't bad visibility as I remember seeing it fly by.

Wednesday 4ᵗʰ November 1953
Page 164 of "Northumberland Aviation Diary"

Meteor F8 WK886 254 Sqd RAF Horsham-St-Faith. While detached to RAF Acklington it dived into the sea 15 mile east of Acklington killing the pilot, possibly after canopy hit target tow cable.

1954

Friday 19th February 1954

DH89 Rapide G-AFMF. Took off from Woolsington Airport on a charter flight to Dublin in order to transport a seven man boxing team from Durham University.

Soon after take off, icing up was encountered and the plane eventually crashed and burst into flames on Stooprigg Fell, near Simonburn, north of Hexham. Incredibly there were no fatalities

Extract from "Hexham Courant"

Pilot Saved the Day for Crash Victims, Assisted in Rescue from Blazing Plane Despite Injury.

Ex-bomber pilot, 31 year old Brian Waugh from Darras Hall really saved the day for his passengers when his plane crashed and burst into flames on Stooprigg Fell, four mile from Simonburn on Friday morning.

The pilot brought the plane down in swirling mist to make a soft landing on level moorland, but in spite of the fact he had a broken ankle – he assisted the passengers from the burning plane to the nearest farmhouse.

The seven passengers in the twin DH Rapide biplane which was on its way from Woolsington to Dublin with members of Durham University Boxing Team, was to have competed with eleven other teams in the University Boxing Championships in Dublin on Friday.

Only fifteen minutes after the plane had taken off from Woolsington and when at 3,000 feet, ice formed on the paravanes. The pilot decided to return to Newcastle but was unable to turn the plane and had to crash-land it on open country. Great holes were torn in the fuselage and nose but none of the passengers was seriously injured.

The nearest farm was more than one mile away from the crash. Firemen, Police and three Ambulances were guided across the fells by farmer Jim Nicholson and some of the University Students, but the ambulances were unable to reach the plane so firemen, police and ambulance men had to carry some of the injured almost two mile across the fells on stretchers to the ambulances which took the pilot and all the passengers to Hexham General Hospital. All were treated for shock but four were detained.

Sub Officer E. Harris of the Hexham Fire Service said that when they reached the plane it was just a smouldering mass of twisted metal. He said the occupants of the plane have had a remarkable escape.

Note :- The aircraft was piloted by Mr Brian Waugh who, through this incident, was to become the first commercial pilot to be charged in a civil court after an air crash. Mr Waugh was found guilty of being responsible for controls icing up and causing the resulting crash. He was fined £50.

His son Richard now living in New Zealand has written a book, " Turbulent Years. A Commercial Pilot's Story", explaining how his father was wrongly convicted.

Further note:- The author while a member of Northumberland Fire Brigade served at Hexham for several years under Sub Officer E. Harris.

Friday 27th March 1954

Vampire FB5 VZ115 608 Sqd RAF Ouston. Collided with 607 Sqd Vampire VZ838 in a turn and was forced to belly-land back at base.

Pilot:- S/Ldr J.A.Stephen

Saturday 30th October 1954

Meteor T7 WH225 607 Sqd RAF Ouston. Yawed (slewed) on overshoot and wing hit the ground causing the aircraft to break up.

Pilot :- F/L W. Hester

1955

Friday 1st April 1955
Page 164 of "Northumberland Aviation Diary"

Chipmunk Mk.T 10 WP780 Durham UAS RAF Ouston, hit a spectator stand during a low-level display and cartwheeled killing 6 spectators, 6 mile north of Otterburn. Pilot was not seriously injured.

Sunday 24th May 1955

Vampire T11 XE832 4 FTS RAF Middleton-St-George. Abandoned near Stocksfield after false fire warning.

Sunday 11th September 1955

Taylorcraft Auster Mk.V1 TW 582 1969 Flight 664 Sqd RAF Usworth. Stalled after an over run of airstrip and dived into the ground near Otterburn, killing the pilot.

1956

Saturday 21st January 1956

Vampire FB5 WA449 607 Sqd RAF Ouston. Hit slipstream on formation take-off causing the wing to hit the ground. Pilot:- P/O C. Lutman.

1957

Thursday 8th August 1957
Page 164 of "Northumberland Aviation Diary"

G. Meteor Mk.T7 VW 488 13 Group Communications Flight RAF Ouston. Dived into the ground after take-off 1 mile WNW of Belsay.

Crew :- 2 killed.

1909114 Sgt. J.J. Cox RAF age 32 Grave at St. Mary's cemetery Stamfordham.

Friday 13th December 1957

Hunter F6 XG202 66 Sqd RAF Acklington. Engine flamed out and aircraft was abandoned 1¼ mile NNE of Morpeth as ASI (Air Speed Indicator) was not working.

1958

Friday 14ᵗʰ February 1958
0930hrs
　　Hunter F6 XG236 66 Sqd RAF Acklington. T/o on high level sortie to practice instrument flying as pilot only completed his instrument rating exam: one week earlier. He then flew down coast to Middlesbrough and turned inland to Kielder. Carried out a mock attack on another Hunter at 40,000ft and followed it into cloud in a high-speed dive.

　　Suspected failure of the elevator actuator resulted in the dive becoming steeper. The aircraft was in the process of pulling up when it struck a hilltop 1,200ft above sea level north of Wainhope near Kielder Reservoir, Northumberland, burying itself in boggy land killing the pilot :-
F/O B.W. Schooling age 23 Grave at Broomhill.

　　This site was excavated in 2001 by Jim Corbett, small items were recovered.

1961

Saturday 5ᵗʰ August 1961
　　Whirlwind HAR4 XL113 228 Sqd RAF Acklington. Engine cut during winching practice, ditched and sank in Cullercoats Bay, Northumberland.

Monday 4ᵗʰ September 1961
Page 165 of "Northumberland Aviation Diary"
　　Vampire T11 XD592 1 FTS RAF Linton-on-Ouse. Lost radio aids; unable to locate base and abandoned out of fuel 7 mile NNW of Acklington.

1962

Tuesday 27ᵗʰ March 1962
　　Jet Provost T3 XN599 6FTS RAF Acklington. Swung off runway on landing and skidded into a bank-side.

Tuesday 8ᵗʰ May 1962
　　Jet Provost T3 XM422 6 FTS RAF Acklington. Flew into ground during display practice, ½ mile WSW of Acklington. Both pilots killed.
　　F/Lt D.D. Wyman age 30 Grave at Broomhill
Mr R C Fenwick stated - *"Farm hands from nearby Cheeveley Farm rushed to the scene but 2 crew were burnt alive."*

Wednesday 9ᵗʰ May 1962
　　Jet Provost T3 XN604 6 FTS Abandoned after false fire warning 5 mile south of Acklington

Friday 18th May 1962

Javelin **FAW9** XH755 33 Sqd RAF Middleton-St-George. Control lost and abandoned in spin 7 mile east of Tynemouth killing the pilot.

Tuesday 14th August 1962

Provost T1 XF684 of 6 FTS RAF Acklington collided with Provost XF903 of same unit while overshooting RLG (Reserve Landing Ground) at Ouston at night. Both pilots killed.

P/O JF Thomas age 21 is buried at Stamfordham.

Tuesday 16th October 1962

Jet Provost T3 AN601 6 FTS RAF Acklington. Lost power on take-off and hit the ground ½ mile west of base.

1963

Thursday 18th April 1963

Jet Provost T4 XP635 6 FTS RAF Acklington. Fire warning light caused the aircraft to be abandoned 2 mile E of Netherwitton, at Whitton Shields. Crew bailed out.

F/L B Shadbolt	Pilot	minor injuries.
P/O Gladwin	Pupil Pilot	OK

1965

Thursday 29th July 1965

Jet Provost T3 XN603 6 FTS RAF Acklington. Abandoned on approach 2 mile SW of base after false fire warning.

1970

Tuesday 6th October 1970

Harrier GR1 XV796 1 Sqd RAF Wittering. Engine flamed out on approach – was abandoned and crashed in field near Ouston. This was first squadron Hunter to crash.

1972

Friday 7th July 1972

Sioux AH1 XT114 AAC. Crashed at Otterburn and burnt out during "Operation Skywarrior."

1977

Saturday 30th July 1977
Page 165 of "Northumberland Aviation Diary"

   Jaguar Mk.T2 XX148 226 OCU RAF Lossiemouth. Inverted and dived into the ground during low-level attack exercise near Whittingham Station, Bridge-of-Aln Hotel, six mile west of Alnwick killing both crew members.

F/Lt J Hinchcliff	Pilot
F/O R Graham	Pupil Pilot

Letter from Mr Tony Brown :- *My father came on the Jaguar crash at Whittingham Station just after it happened and had seen it suddenly pull up before diving into the ground. His impression was that it had been a bird striking the cockpit and a natural pilot reaction to the impact. The plane had impacted the ground in a near vertical dive and was totally buried.*

1983

Wednesday 13th April 1983

   Starfighter Mk.F104G D-8337 312 Sqd (Dutch) RNAF Volkel was detached to RAF Connonsby for NATO Exercise "Mallet Blow". It was in a flight of two when the aircraft was homing in on target but then looped and went into a steep dive into the ground at Ridlees Hope, 3 mile west of Alwinton.

Here is D-8337 seen prior to it's crash near Alwinton. (Theo Stoelinger)

   Crew :- 2nd Lt M. Sasbrink-Harkema (Dutch) age 26 Managed to eject but was killed.

1984

Sunday 2nd December 1984

Page 165 of "Northumberland Aviation Diary"

   Piper Aztec. From possibly Austria, was on a delivery flight to America via Reykjavik, Iceland when it attempted to land at Newcastle Airport to refuel, but in thick fog it crashed short of the runway at Black Callerton Farm, Northumberland. The pilot an Austrian was found dead in the wreckage.

Remains of Piper Aztec at Black Callerton.

1985

Thursday 24th October 1985
Page 165 of "Northumberland Aviation Diary"
1530hrs

Tornado IDS 4145 (44+45) JBG-32 Fighter Bomber Wing 32 German Air Force was on exercise "Mallet Blow" in thick fog. The aircraft had flown from its base in Germany and carried out one low level mock attack on the target area at Otterburn, it then refueled at an

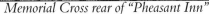
Memorial Cross rear of "Pheasant Inn"

Area of crash in far background.

RAF base and was in the process of a second attack when it struck the ground about 300 yards above the "Pheasant Inn", at Dykeman`s Edge, Stannersburn, Kielder, killing both crew.:-

Hptmn Hans Joachim Schimpf Pilot GAF Killed
Hptmn Holgar Zacharias Nav GAF Killed

1987

Monday 2nd November 1987
Page 166 of "Northumberland Aviation Diary"

Two **Harriers GR3** XZ136 and GR3 XV790 of 3 Sqd RAF Guttersloh, Germany, were taking part in a 6 aircraft co-ordinated attack (operation "Mallet Blow") on the Otterburn SAM site, but collided over the target and crashed two kilometers apart near Rotten Crag, in the Riddles Hope area of Redesdale. An eyewitness said, "The fighters flew in low from different angles and collided. The tail section of one split away and it spun into the ground exploding in a huge fireball". The pilot made no attempt to eject. The other pilot ejected shortly before impact with the ground but too late for the seat to complete its sequence.
Both pilots were killed, one was from the US Navy.

1989

Friday 21st July 1989
Page 166 of "Northumberland Aviation Diary"

Tornado F3 XE833 23 Sqd RAF Leeming. Lost height in low level interception and abandoned, crashing into the sea 35 mile NE of Tynemouth while on a training exercise. The crew bailed out and the navigator was rescued by Sea King from Boulmer and was taken to Newcastle suffering from hypothermia. The pilot who came originally from Glasgow, was married and living in Northallerton, drowned while trapped in his parachute under his dinghy.

Crew :-

F/Lt	Stephen Moir	Pilot	age 28	drowned
		Navigator		bailed out successfully

1990

Tuesday 9ᵗʰ January 1990
Page 167 of "Northumberland Aviation Diary"

Tornado GR1 ZA394 2 Sqd Army Co-Op RAF Laarbruch Germany. Collided with Jaguar XZ 108 during practice attack on Spadeadam Ranges and lost control at low altitude and abandoned. They had refueled at RAF Wattisham and were flying around Britain to go out via Leeming when they collided with a Jaguar and crashed at Styford Bridge, near Riding Mill Roundabout, Northumberland. The Tornado crew bailed out but in doing so injured their legs and were taken to Hospital by helicopter from RAF Boulmer. The mother-in-law of the Navigator Mrs Joyce lives at Dalton, Greenhead, Northumberland.

Crew :-

F/Lt	Ian MacLean	Pilot	Bailed out - one broken leg.
F/Lt	Neil Johnston	Nav	Bailed out - two broken legs.

1991

10ᵗʰ April 1991

Skylark 3 Glider of Borders Gliding Club, Milfield crashed on take-off.

Letter from Mr Gerry Newman :- *"The accident happened just after take-off in very turbulent conditions – the rope detached from the aircraft leaving me with few options – having missed the old RAF Milfield buildings and a power line by a very small margin, I crashed into a small stand of conifers (roughly where the new entrance to the Gliding Club now is) during*

Mr Gerry Newman and wrecked glider.

the impact the aircraft swung round 180 degs and came to rest on a small road, having shed various items, including the tail. The club members who witnessed the accident were convinced that I would be dead (I'm still not sure if they were disappointed to find me standing next to the wreckage)!! I still fly at Milfield as a tug pilot every three weeks or so."

1992

16th July 1992
Page 167 of "Northumberland Aviation Diary"

Two **Tornado F3**s while training at 2,000 feet collided over Wooler. The tail of one jet striking the underside of the other causing minor damage to both. No crews were injured. Both aircraft landed at Newcastle Airport for checks.

1993

Tuesday 18th October 1993
Page 167 of "Northumberland Aviation Diary"
1050hrs

Cadet III G-BRVJ of Brian Outhwait.

Piper Cherokee G-BRJV in field near Dinnington.

Cadet 111 G-BRVJ (Should read):- Piper Cherokee G-BRJV was on a training flight from Newcastle when the pilot Mr Ronald Thompson of 58, Briery Hill Cottage, Stannington, was forced to make an emergency landing on a bridal path in a field between Dinnington and Seaton Burn. The pilot was unhurt.

Please Note:-My apologies go to Mr Brian Outhwaite for my wrongly recording his Cadet 111 G-BRVJ as G-BRJV, as being the aircraft involved in this incident, - which incidentally was not airborne that day. Photographs display the difference of aircraft.

November 1993
Famous Woman Pilot Dies

Miss Constance (Connie) Ruth Leathart, whose home was near Capheaton in North Northumberland died aged 89. She was considered one of the country's foremost women pilots in the 1920's.

A pioneering member of the Cramlington-based Newcastle Aero Club, she went on to establish herself in European air racing, rallies and aero events.

During WW2 the ATA (Air Transport Auxiliary) was formed to assist the RAF with movement of aircraft, this was on a non-operational flying bases.

Miss Leathart was among some of the earliest aviators to volunteer for this venture. She joined on 14th August 1940 and rose to the rank of Flight Captain, which allowed her to fly all types of aircraft including the four engined heavy bombers.

On one occasion on 6th January 1941 while in transit, Connie shared a room at RAF Squires Gate near Blackpool with Amy Johnson, the night before the famous flyer was killed

On the disbandment of ATA towards the end of WW2 Connie retired from the service on 30th June 1944, although she still flew privately with her own plane until 1958.

1995

Monday 30th October 1995
Page 170 of "Northumberland Aviation Diary"
2000 hrs

Tornado F3 ZE773 43 Sqd RAF Leuchars. Collided with Tornado ZE210 of the same unit while formating on each other and was abandoned 56 mile NE of Berwick-upon-Tweed. The crew of ZE773 ejected safely and were picked up by a helicopter from RAF Boulmer. Two weeks later the Starboard undercarriage door from this aircraft washed up on the beach in front of Bamburgh Castle, where it is now on display with the kind permission of Commanding Officer RAF Leuchars.

Tornado ZE210 sustained serious damage to the port side but the crew, with great difficulty, were able to regain control and return to base.

1999

Saturday 23th January 1999

Pegasus Glider Crash landed at Milfield aerodrome. The pilot 65 year old Mr Julian Sutton, a former commercial pilot, was trapped in the cockpit until extracted from the wreckage. He needed hospital treatment so was flown by helicopter to Ashington Hospital before being transferred to Newcastle General Hospital for his back and leg injuries.

Wednesday 14th July 1999
Page 171 of "Northumberland Aviation Diary"
1430hrs

Harrier GR7 ZG532 from RAF Cottesmore crashed in a field and exploded near Pallinsburn House, Cornhill-on-Tweed. When at 400 feet, pilot ejected and came down in a wooded area nearby where he was suspended in a tree and managed to cut himself free. He was subsequently taken to the Borders General Hospital with slight injuries for a check up.

1330 hrs

SOCATA Tobago TB 10 G-BHER The pilot, a member of Newcastle Aero Club decided to make an emergency landing on the beach at Druridge Bay as the engine was running a bit rough. After a successful landing the pilot and passenger were able to climb out of the plane unhurt.

Coastguards helped to pull the aeroplane clear of high water mark where it could be guarded until an engineer could be called The aircraft was able to take-off from the beach next day at 1120 hrs.

Tobago on beach.

Saturday 14th August 1999
Page 171 of "Northumberland Aviation Diary"

1740 hrs

Europa crash.

Account taken from "Northumberland Gazette"

A plane crash has left a man in hospital with injuries to his face and chest.

The crash happened on the runway of Brunton airfield. A spokesman for the airfield said that as the two seater Europa taxied along the runway preparing to take-off, the right control cable appeared to have snapped, sending the plane off to the left and through the wire fence into the woods.

The pilot and his male passenger, who have not been named are thought to be local farmers and although both were admitted to hospital, the passenger has been released without treatment. The pilot was detained in Wansbeck Hospital, although his injuries are not thought to be life threatening.

Thursday 14th October 1999
Page 171 of "Northumberland Aviation Diary"

Tornado GR4 ZD809 of 14 Sqd RAF Lossiemouth. Was one of two aircraft descending from seaward over Coquet Island en-route to an exercise at Spadeadam. It crashed near Wallridge, 3½ mile NW of Stamfordham. The aircraft was seen at approx:150 feet, seconds before it dived into the ground in a huge fireball spreading debris over 400 yards (metres) and killing both crew who were from 15(R) Sqd.

| F/Lt | R. A. | Wright. | Pilot | age 30 from Wolverhampton |
| F/Lt | S. P. | Casabayo. | Nav | age 30 from Plymouth |

Note:- It is thought the accident happened after the crew of the low flying Tornado became unsure of their position in poor weather and visibility and were trying to change course away from air space controlled by Newcastle Airport.

As the plane attempted to bank sharply away from the area, it went into a steep descent and crashed at Wallridge near Ingoe.

2000

Wednesday 18th October 2000
1640 hrs

    H S Hawk 100 Sqd of RAF Leeming crashed when on a training exercise 1½ mile north east of Lowick with the ejected crew landing one mile west of their aircraft.

    The aircraft was coming in from the sea when a bird shattered the canopy. The pilot then pulled up into a sharp vertical climb with the engine losing power. The aircraft flipped over on to its back and started to dive into the ground as the crew ejected. It then bounced over a hedge and blew up causing a fire, which totally wrecked the remains. The crew were a F/Lt Instructor and a pupil navigator who were not seriously injured.

Wednesday 29th November 2000
Evening

    Jabiru UL G - RODG A two seater enclosed microlight, with fixed high wing, is an Australian kit built aircraft costing about £20,000, crashed on landing in a field at Bockenfield near Eshott airfield. The pilot Mr Roger Rhodes aged 56, a member of Eshott Flying Club, stated that the engine failed at 400 feet and refused to restart while coming in to land. To avoid obstructions he decided to put

Jabiru in field near Eshott.

down in a field adjacent to the airfield. Unfortunately the nose wheel dug into the soft surface and the aircraft turned over onto its roof. Both occupants were able to crawl from the wreckage. The male passenger 23 year old Terry Mason suffered head cuts, bruising, and injuries to his chest and legs. The pilot sustained only whiplash injuries. They were both taken to Ashington's Wansbeck Hospital where the pilot was allowed to go home after treatment.

The Air Accident Investigation Branch report stated, the engine had stopped due to severe carburettor icing up.

2002

Sunday 28th April 2002
1340 hrs

Grumman AA5 crash at Stainton Airstrip.

Grumman AA-5. Of the Echo Oscar Flying Group syndicate, crashed on landing at a private airstrip at Selby Farm, Stanton near Morpeth. It clipped a tree then crashed through a wall and crossed a road before coming to rest in a field. The four-seater plane was en-route from Teesside Airport to Eshott Airfield near Felton. It is believed a strong and sudden gust of wind caused it to clip a tree. The pilot Mr Nick Lyons and his male passenger were injured and taken to Wansbeck General Hospital, but only the pilot was detained overnight.

2003

Friday 30th May 2003
1515 hrs

Bell Jet Ranger Helicopter. Was being used by BBC for a film "Britain Through Time" with presenter Alan Titmarsh. It crashed at Sycamore Gap near Edges Green, north of Once Brewed Pub above Haltwhistle, and is said to have occurred when the

Crashed Helicopter at Edges Green.

Helicopter was about 200 feet high and was making a turn, when it yawed to the right. The pilot tried to correct the turn, but realised the helicopter was out of control and decided he had no choice but to crash land.

On board was a film crew taking pictures of Alan on the Roman Wall. All three in the helicopter were able to jump clear as it crashed onto its side.

2004

Thursday 22nd July 2004
1100hrs

Tornado GR4 from RAF Marham. While flying at low level the aircraft dived into the sea 7 mile east of Low Newton-by-the-Sea. The two crew ejected only seconds before the crash. They were picked up from the sea floating in their dinghy within 25 minutes, by 202 Sqd Sea King from RAF Boulmer and taken to hospital with minor injuries or check up.

2005

Thursday 10th March 2005
1730 hrs

Robinson R44 Helicopter. Crashed while making landing in the grounds of Langley Castle. The helicopter tipped over on touching down and caught fire, the pilot and two passengers were able to scramble clear of the wreckage before the arrival of fire appliances from Haydon Bridge, Hexham and Allendale.

Airfields in Northumberland

RAF Ouston
Letter from Mr Eric Nicholson

Page 179 of your book tells us of the history of RAF Ouston. I was stationed there in the Autumn of 1946 along with F/O Johnson, we two were Liaison Signal Section with F.A.A. (Fleet Air Arm).

There were four French airwoman in the section and I would go in first thing in a morning and often be greeted with "The teleteep — it go Brrrrr ! Brrrrr— the teleteep." Well I would solve whatever the problem was and all the many other mysteries of English/RAF procedure and over the few months the girls and I were great friends.

There is a very sad ending to this story as all four ladies returned to France and within weeks they were killed in a train crash.

What follows is perfectly true — it reads I would think, a bit far fetched, but it happened.

Very many years later, I was travelling in a train from Newcastle Central to York. A young soldier was sitting opposite me and — unusual for Englishmen on a train !— we got chatting. He revealed he was stationed at the Albermarle Barracks which had once been RAF Ouston. I was alerted – and some !! He was working in what was or had been, the old Signal Section and was not all that happy working there, nor were other fellow soldiers with him. It appears from time to time they would hear sounds of French speaking women – words could not be understood but he gathered at one time some French "WAAFS" had been stationed there!!! I did not tell my young companion of my association with Ouston, the Signal Section or the French sounds.

RAF Morpeth
Letter from Mr Eric Nicholson

Mentioned in page 178 of your book, I knew this station as RAF Tranwell. I was an Air Training Corps youngster who had been able to spend several days there and got the opportunity to fly in Bothas. I had two trips sitting beside the pilot and watching barrels being attacked in the North Sea. One of these pilots was a "resting" Battle of Britain man and the other was a Polish airman (my second flight) and we wound up in a ploughed field on return – unhurt – undamaged.

Note:- (Author:- 17th March 1943, Botha W5140 of 4 AGS crashed on landing).

Other Installations

Page 182 of "Northumberland Aviation Diary"

Further information on:-
Ack-Ack and Searchlight installations

410 Battery, 537 Searchlight Reg: (5th Royal Northumberland Fusiliers T.A)

H.Q at Rock Hall but later moved to Heaton, Debdon Gardens.

Cluster sites of 3 – 150cm searchlights linked together and often accompanied by Heavy or medium Ack-Ack. Some sites were situated as follows:-

Shipley and Eglingham NW of Alnwick.

Brunton, near airfield.

Berwick Cricket Field. (Pavilion used as accommodation).

Border Bridge Bofus Guns
Tweedmouth on hill above
Scremerston on sloping fields near old house, was a line of three Radar Controlled searchlights with 3 heavy Ack-Ack guns behind
Benwell near West road just past Milvain Club
Dissington
Gosforth (City Golf Course)
Morpeth, Stobhill
Woolsingham

Heavy Ack Ack sites also at :-
Longbenton opposite Bridle Path Golf Course.
Wallsend, Churchhill St.
Blyth
Tynemouth Rocket Site near Park Hotel

Poets Corner

This section contains a selection of authors favourite aviation poems.

To A Bomber Pilot

Take down his coat,
Pick up his things,
The scribbled note,
The tunic with wings;
The book, Cricket pads and bat
And his beloved Mis-shapen Hat,

Auction his car,
Attend to his Debts,
And then there are
His several Pets-
The Tortoise, Collie Dog and bird,
Whose cheerful chirp is now unheard,

No more kissing
And Popsies thrilled;
He's reported "Missing,
Believed Killed",
He had no Ribbons, Won no Fame;
We'll toast his memory just the same.

By Vernon Noble.
RAF Linton-on-Ouse, 1941

Derek

I saw you glistening in the sky
Like gleaming vapour flashing by,
I saw you next upon a marble shelf
A scorched grotesqueness of yourself,
The house you hit was still a smouldering shell
That storm we had has turned my life to hell.

I went along to see
What could be done-
The smell of singeing flesh
And jagged, ugly hunks of metal
Still remained.

The wheels were there, and bricks
And burnt-up privet hedges,
A single yellow rose
Was blooming on a blackened stem,
I stood and looked and wept
My heart cried out to Him.

And as I stood, a little man
Came up and watched as well
"Your house, Ma'am? And your garden, Ma'am?
It will all grow again…
But when I turned and looked at him
Just then he understood.
He picked the rose and gave it me
"I'm sorry, very sorry, Ma'am, I didn't know," he said,
"Someone I love," I cried,
My heart sighs out for him,

The years have passed,
My searing pains remained,
I went along again to look
And there, as in a dream,
A house of Phoenix stood,
Agleam and clean, with bright blue paint.
(The yellow rose was there)
And underneath the hedge
Of privet lay a puppy
And a battered teddybear, and close by
Stood a pram.
"Life for a Life," I cried,
And wept for freedom from my Calvery.

This poem was written by Air Transport Auxiliary pilot Diana Barnato Walker (left picture) after the death of her husband Wing Commander Derek Walker, (right picture) when his Mustang F4. KM232 stalled recovering from a dive out of cloud and spun into a house at Finchley, Middlesex on 14th November 1945.

Requiem for an Air Gunner.

The pain has stopped,
For I am dead,
My time on earth is done,
But in a hundred years from now,
I'll still be twenty-one,

My brief sweet life is over,
My eyes no longer see,
No summer walks,
No Christmas trees,
No pretty girls for me,

I've got the chop, I've had it,
My nightly ops; are done,
Yet in a hundred years,
I'll still be twenty-one.

R.W. Gilbert

An Airman's Prayer.

My God , this night I have to fly
And ere I leave the ground
I come with reverence to Thy Throne
Where perfect peace is found

I thank Thee for the life I've had
For home and all its love
I thank Thee for the faith I have
That cometh from above

Come with me now into the air
Be with me as I fly
Guide Thou each move that I shall make
Way up there in the sky

Be with me at the target, Lord
When danger's at its height
Be with me as I drop my load
And on the homeward flight

And should it be my turn to die
Be with me to the end
Help me to die a Christian's death
On Thee, God I depend

Then as I leave this mortal frame
From human ties set free
Receive my soul, O God of Love
I humbly come to Thee.

Written by South African Eric Impey, the day before he died in his Liberator over Warsaw, while delivering supplies to the Polish uprising in that area on 16th August 1944.

"Hurricane, 1940"

Just twisted scrap thrown on a dump
Strips of wing and a Merlin sump
Old fighter plane
Your flight is done
Your landings made and the victories won

Gun barrels scorched and motor's tired
Your masters fought as men inspired
Old fighter plane
They trusted you
Who faithfully served the Gallant Few

Casually now they fly around
Jet propelled at speed of sound
New fighter planes
Fierce in your power
Spare thought for those who had their hour.

Harold Balfour

"For Johnny"

Do not despair
For Johnny headin-air;
He sleeps as sound
As Johnny under ground

Fetch out no shroud
For Johnny in the cloud;
And keep your tears
For him in after years

Better by far
For Johnny the bright star,
To keep your head,
And see his children fed.

John Pudney

Stumpy

Stumpy and his wife Martha went to the State Fair every year.
Every year Stumpy would say, "Martha, – I'd like to ride in that there airplane"

And every year Martha would say, "I know Stumpy, but that airplane ride costs ten dollars, and ten dollars is ten dollars."

One year Stumpy and Martha went to the fair and Stumpy said, "Martha I'm 71 years old, if I don't ride that airplane this year I may never get another chance."

Martha replied, "Stumpy, that there airplane ride costs ten dollars, and ten dollars is ten dollars."

The pilot overheard them and said, "Folks, I'll make you a deal,
I'll take you both up for a ride, and if you can stay quiet for the entire ride and not say one word, I won't charge you, but if you say one word, it's ten dollars."

Stumpy and Martha agreed and up they go. The pilot does all kinds of twists and turns, rolls and dives, but not a word is heard.
He does all his tricks over again, but not a word.

They land and the pilot turns to Stumpy. "By golly, I did everything I could think of to get you to yell out, but you didn't."

Stumpy replied, "Well, I was gonna say something when Martha fell out, but ten dollars is ten dollars."

The author received this amusing tale from friend and pilot Don Puls of Chicago.

High Flight

Oh! I have slipped the surly bonds of Earth
And danced the skies on laughter silvered wings;
Sunward I've climbed, and joined the tumbling mirth
Of sun-split clouds – and done a hundred things
You have not dreamed of – wheeled and soared and swung
High in the sunlit silence. Hov'ring there,
I've chased the shouting wind along, and flung
My eager craft through footless halls of air…
Up, up the long, delirious burning blue
I've topped the wind-swept heights with easy grace,
Where never lark, or even eagle flew –
And, while with silent, lifting mind I've trod
The high untrespassed sanctity of space,
Put out my hand and touched the face of God.

John Gillespie Magee

P/O John Magee.

Until late 1995 my wife and I ran a 'Bed & Breakfast' service from our home in Bamburgh. In the visitors lounge we had a copy of the poem 'High Flight' hanging on the wall.

One evening a couple booked in for one night. Next morning on leaving the lady told me she had known John Gillespie Magee personally. Her father had been the Headmaster at Rugby school where John was a pupil. Being so far from home, her father and the family had taken him 'under their wing' by making him welcome in their home and including him in family holidays. They became firm friends. She also stated that John had written a book of poetry. (Later I was to learn from this book, which included a biography of John written by Stephen Garnett,- that the lady who stayed overnight was Elinor Lyon daughter of the headmaster, and I suspect that John and her were at one time sweethearts.) Copies of this book can be obtained from "This England Books" ISBN 0 906324 10 6. – P.O.Box 52, Cheltenham, Gloucestershire, GL50 1YQ.

John Gillespie Magee was born in Shanghai on 9th June 1922. He was the first of four sons born to Faith and John Magee working as American missionaries in China.

Faith was the daughter of Rev. Backhouse the Rector of Helmingham in Suffolk

The parents had planned that when their sons were old enough they would send them to school in England then to America to finish their education.

In November 1931 after attending school in Nanking for three years, John was enrolled as a pupil at St. Clare's boarding school, near Walmer, Kent. It was during his last year at Clare's that he started to write poetry.

In 1935 he moved to Rugby's famous public school where in 1939 he won the coveted Rugby Poetry Prize. In the summer of that year his parents persuaded him to go to America in order to complete his education. This he did reluctantly and when war broke out he felt that he had deserted England, the land he loved so well.

He endeavoured to obtain a passport to return but the American State Department refused as he was too young. Although ensured of a place at Yale University, he persuaded his parents to allow him to join the Royal Canadian Air Force, and at the end of March 1941 he was posted to the Service Flying School at Uplands, Ontario, making his first solo flight after only six hours flying time. He gained his wings in June 1941.

On being posted to England his first flight in a Spitfire took place on 7th August 1941 and afterwards in the mess while rapturously singing the praises of the aircraft, a fellow pilot suggested he should put his thoughts into words. This he did there and then by composing the poem 'High Flight' on the inside of a cigarette packet.

September 1941 found him in the all Canadian 412 Spitfire Squadron at Wellingore, Lincolnshire (a satellite of Digby) where he was a very popular figure, enjoying the comradeship that existed amongst the members of the Squadron.

On 11th December 1941 during a Squadron formation flight the Spitfires were letting down through cloud south east of Wellingore. It was then John's aircraft (Serial No. AD 291) collided with an Airspeed Oxford aircraft which was on a training flight in the vicinity of its base at RAF Cranwell. The pupil pilot, who was the sole occupant, LAC E. A. Griffin, failed to bale out and both aircraft plunged to the ground half a mile apart. An eyewitness to the collision reported that John seemed to have difficulty baling out of his aircraft and this resulted in him being too near the ground for his parachute to open. Both the young pilots were unfortunately killed.

As John was one of the first casualties to a Washington family in WW2, (America had only just entered the war four days before this with the Japanese bombing of Pearl Harbour) the American newspapers carried the story of his death together with his poem 'High Flight' a copy of which had been obtained from John's father.

The poem so captured the imagination of the American people and soon spread to the Canadian and British newspapers. In the aftermath of the American space shuttle disaster in 1986 President Reagan in a nation-wide broadcast quoted a few lines from 'High flight' as a tribute to the ill-fated Challenger crew.

'High Flight' is now regarded as a classic piece of War Poetry and is known as the anthem for flyers everywhere. The original manuscript has been placed in the Library of Congress at Washington.

John Gillespie Magee age nineteen years, was buried in Scopwick cemetery, Lincolnshire. The first and last lines of his poem 'High flight' are engraved on his headstone.